JESUS
AND THE
MENNONITES

JESUS

AND THE

MENNONITES

A Call to Reclaim the Spirit of Amish Evangelism

by Hector Troyer

Jesus and the Mennonites
First edition.

Copyright © 2023 Hector Troyer. All rights reserved.

No part of this publication may be reproduced, distributed, or transmitted in any form or by any means, including photocopying, recording, or other electronic or mechanical methods, without the prior written permission of the publisher, except in the case of brief quotations embodied in reviews and certain other non-commercial uses permitted by copyright law.

Scripture taken from the New King James Version®. Copyright © 1982 by Thomas Nelson. Used by permission. All rights reserved.

This book is intended to be prophetic and not prescriptive in nature. This book represents the views, opinions, and biases of the author. The ideas in this book are intended to generate serious thought and discussion about our approach to missions. This book is not intended to represent the views or opinions held by all Anabaptists. This book is not intended to be a manual on church planting. The author is not claiming perfection or mastery in any of the mentioned areas.

Published by S2S Books, Granby, MA, strengthtostrength.org.

ISBN: 979-8-9893147-1-3
Printed in the United States of America.

TABLE OF CONTENTS

Foreword iii
Introduction vii
Critical Cultural Shift
    1. Holy Hermeneutics 3
    2. Slippery Salvation 7
    3. Twice the Son of Hell 11
Vision Casting
    4. Begin with the End in Mind 17
    5. Change Your Mind About Mission 21
    6. Simple Math 25
    7. Look What Worked 31
Comfort Crisis
    8. Comfort Mindset 39
    9. Consumer Churches 43
    10. Risk Aversion 49
    11. Opportunity Cost 53

Strategies for Conquest
    12. Empower Your People 59
    13. Don't Go Alone 65
    14. Become Native 69
    15. Think Logistics 73

And Now…
    16. Powerful Prayer 83
    17. Do It 87

Afterword 89
Recommended Resources 91

FOREWORD

  Ideas have consequences. We can try to deny it, but the philosophy and habits of our lives determine our future and greatly influence that of our children. The sad thing is that too often, we don't realize we have the wrong ideas until it's too late. This is true not only of individuals but of whole church communities. We all naturally prefer flattery, but when we finally get old enough to appreciate the truth, it's often sadly too late. Whether it's the doctor, accountant, or good Christian friend, the truth is good for us—even if it hurts.

  Hector Troyer, in this book, *Jesus and the Mennonites*, offers several challenging ideas. His central idea is the expansion of the Kingdom of God through healthy, planned, intentional church division. Just as in the human body, healthy cells should constantly be dividing naturally in order to create new cells; this is also true of a healthy church. When we don't have this,

Foreword

things are off somewhere. In the human body, lots can go wrong. Toxins, disease, and neglect kill our healthy cells. The church is no different. Hector hits a few of those toxic ideas that can vex the church. Some of his cures may be challenging. Don't let that scare you off. Like a good doctor, I suggest allowing Hector's ideas to challenge your spiritual thinking. There could be a reason why you and your family—or church—haven't been feeling well lately.

When it comes to picking a doctor, or an accountant for that matter, we don't want a quack or a novice. I'm not interested in someone using unethical practices or trying to make a name for themselves. If you're going to let someone into your most intimate spaces, you want to know that they are professional and well-grounded in a body of ideas that are tested and have shown evidence of fruitfulness.

Here is where Hector stands out. While Hector brings challenges, he does so in a respectful way, appreciating those who have gone before him. I've sat at the table of many spiritual practitioners. Sad to say, most are pretty apt at diagnosing what's wrong. Few, however, seem able to identify examples of things that work. Hector makes no apology for identifying as an Anabaptist. Hector is unique in that he is able to appreciate the good in the conservative Anabaptists while still striving for more. Surveying uncommon fields, Hector draws our attention to the Amish and other conservative congregations as examples of valuable areas of practice that the more progressive churches have left behind. This is no small accomplishment.

Too often today, in their zeal to make a name for themselves, many coffee table prophets end up tearing down more than they build up. Hector, on the other hand, offers a strong challenge but does so with humility and respect for the contributions of those who have gone before him. It is clear that his desire is to build up the church at large, not to tear it apart. Reading his book, I got the feeling of someone with genuine concerns for the church, not someone who is willing to tear it down to build his own kingdom.

Hector's ideas surrounding a "colonizing" style in missions are radical; pay attention to this section. They are radical, not so much because the ideas are new, but rather because he had the courage to say them out loud. Mission outreach through planned church division is the way Anabaptists have been expanding for centuries. Hector encourages the church to consider these methods, intentionally seeking out places that are best suited for outreach. Hector's book is challenging, but it is a challenge that we need. It is my prayer that the church today can apply many of the things Hector has suggested in this book.

—Dean Taylor
Sugar Creek, Ohio

INTRODUCTION

The main purpose of this book is to *promote intentional church division*. I intend to point out the damage worldly Christianity's view of Jesus is doing to Mennonite culture and faith.

Let's lay the sledgehammer of self-denial to our salty pillars of Babel and make the whole world thirsty. It is time to lay aside our old habit of going with the flow or trying to revive dying congregations and begin to think about what great church division could look like. How could church division be a blessing to the world instead of being a way to further our own selfish agendas? Think about the end. Your church dividing over some petty issue and building another flavor in the same neighborhood would look quite different than your church sending six families to an unchurched area. Think about the end. What if your church was able to send out six families repeatedly? Think about the

Introduction

potential. *What if every Anabaptist church in your area followed this model?* What if they repeated it over and over again?

Some churches may want to send several families to a foreign country. Some would send families to inner cities. Some would send families to remote rural areas. And some churches would recognize that they are operating in an already saturated area, close their doors and relocate the entire group. And what if those new churches did the same thing as they grew?

But before we get too far, let's think about some *attitudes we have borrowed from worldly churches.* Have we lost the vision of *why* the world needs a faithful witness? Are you ready to think long and hard about the why?

In the last twenty-five years I have observed subtle changes in our Anabaptist culture. I am certain that my generation is not the only one to watch cultural shifts. I have puzzled and prayed and wrestled with some of these cultural ideas for a long time. Alone these attitudes seem harmless or even beneficial. But somehow, they are not bearing Galatian fruit.[1] And if several of these attitudes are held in parallel, they rapidly vaporize the New Testament holy living that Anabaptists have historically embodied. It is time to look more critically at what could be causing this subtle shift.

---

[1] Gal. 5:22–23.

Introduction

By writing this short book I do not profess to understand all the interconnected implications of every doctrine. Nor do I claim to be guiltless or to have arrived at some special revelation. Many of these weaknesses are my own. But I want to be vulnerable enough to speak truth that is not always in my favor.

I am pointing out the solution as I see it. I have judged or misjudged each toxic idea or combination of ideas by its own fruit. If you feel bad about judging ideas by their fruit, then you are reading the wrong book — *put it down*. If you feel that everyone who names the name of Jesus is in the same camp, I suggest that you pick up a copy of Darwin's *Origin of the Species* instead.[2]

This book is for you if you love the New Testament holy living that Anabaptists have lived and died for. This book is for you if you are willing to explore inconvenient and uncomfortable implications. If you care about missions and church expansion, this book is for you.

Anabaptism has its problems. We are plagued by greed, gossip and sectarianism. Some of us have forgotten that the world around us exists as we sit and gaze in pharisaical admiration at our own spiritual umbilicus. Most of us are concentrated in a few areas of the continental United States. We are better at being

---

[2] Darwin was a "Christian" who trained to become an Anglican priest.

Introduction

salt blocks than being the salt of the earth. We guard our rusted-out traditions with the ferocity of a junkyard dog. If we wish to gain credibility with the world (and favor with God) we need to work on these problems. But for now, let's think about the ways worldly Christianity has built inroads into our thinking, and look at how that expresses itself in our culture.

"Unless someone like you cares a whole awful lot, nothing is going to get better. It's not."[3]

---

[3] Theodor Geisel (1904–1991).

CRITICAL CULTURAL SHIFT

CHAPTER 1
Holy Hermeneutics

By their fruits you will know them.[1]

Let's start with the basics. How you *think* about how you view the Bible will determine your ability to receive the truth. Do you interpret the Bible through the book of Romans, through the words of Jesus, through the theology of Luther, by the life of early Christians, or through the eyes of an evil English king (James)?

From what bias do you interpret the Bible? He who says he has no bias is a liar and the truth is not in him. Many Christians claim to embrace scripture alone. *What that really means is they are only interested in looking at scripture through their own personal or cultural bias.* We believe that the scriptures are the final uncontested

---

[1] Matt. 7:20.

authority, but we must also acknowledge that we are separated from its authors by thousands of years of history, culture, language, and malicious or ignorant theologians. How else could so many people arrive at wrong conclusions through *Solo Scriptura*?

Everyone, including me, has their biases. We do well to carefully examine our biases and their fruits, to see if we are in the faith. It is not enough to have a bulletproof theology, our Lord Himself gives us the key to understanding theology. He says that *by their fruits you will know them*. Any theology that fails to produce culture wide New Testament holy living is defunct, deceptive, and corrupt. So why are Mennonites borrowing this kind of theology? One good actor does not make a bad theology good. Sure, there will be Catholics and Protestants in Heaven. *So what?* Should we trade a reasonably productive farm for one exceptionally lush flower pot?

Anabaptism is a worldview. It shares some doctrinal components and scriptures with Islam, Mormonism, Catholicism, Jehovah's Witnesses, and Protestantism. But it is distinctly separate from these worldviews. Many Mennonites have forgotten this tidbit. This lack of knowledge has allowed us to wander into the red carpeted halls of ear-tickling theologies that are killing us, destroying New Testament holy living, eroding faith, splitting churches, but mostly kidnapping the young and restless.

Many Mennonite churches are adopting the attitude that the world is getting too smart for under-educated Amish boys. Training is trumping character in the qualifications for spiritual leadership. Seminaries are mostly blinding leaders to lead the blind. They are training the art of manipulation to prospective pastors in the name of protecting church authority. Do we want Gentile leaders for the new Israel? Did anybody remember to read the qualifications for leaders in the New Testament? Did you see seminary training in the list? *By whose definition are the Biblical qualifications not enough?* What happened to the Holy Spirit?

The Anabaptist worldview is distinct in that it relies heavily on Christlike fruits instead of on elaborate theology. We interpret all scripture through the life and example of the living Word, Jesus Christ. We do not need a special Bible version to defend our theology (although some versions are better quality than others). Romans should be no more significant to the Mennonite than what Matthew is. We do not accept the deification of one book. Try defending mainstream worldly theology without using the book of Romans. I am not denigrating Paul's writings. He does a tremendous job of fleshing out the way a Christian should look and live. We listen for the harmony of scripture instead of cherry-picking random words and notes from the gospel song. We do not accept faith without works, but neither do we accept works without faith. The heresy of *sola fide*[2] invented by Martin Luther continues to wreak havoc in worldly Christianity. We hold these fruits to be self-evident that he who is a slave to sin is a slave to sin regardless of his verbal commitment to elaborate theology.

Neither should we be overly impressed by spiritual power. The historical and biblical record is crystal clear about the ability of evil powers to appear as angels of light. Miracles and answered prayers are not clear indicators of God's favor. Exercise great caution when judging groups or individuals that put extra emphasis on the supernatural. You could be dealing with the devil.

Show me the fruit of your theology. I want to see your works. Let your good works be known to all men.[3] What would Jesus *really* do? Would He do the opposite of everything He taught?

---

[2] "faith alone."

[3] Matt. 5:16.

CHAPTER 2
Slippery Salvation

And they will answer Him, "Lord, when did we see You?"[1]

"Are you saved?" What is that question supposed to mean? What are you implying by using this ambiguous (unclear or inexact because a choice between alternatives has not been made) evangelical jargon? Why do we ask people if they are saved? Do you intend to ask if they made some verbal confession of their complete reliance on the righteousness of Jesus? Is that supposed to constitute salvation? Are you asking if they have been baptized, for "by baptism are you saved?"

Worldly Christians point fingers at the Amish and say that they are not "saved." Yet these same people can be all too willing to ignore someone's disobedience

---

[1] Matt. 25:44.

to Jesus' teachings and accept them as brothers on their verbal testimony of what Jesus has done for them. Worldly Christians often define salvation as simply "believing in the finished work of Calvary and accepting Jesus into my heart," and consider any further requirements to be heresy. Of course, there are varying degrees of expectations on how the now-saved person should live, but generally no one may question a person's verbal account of salvation. By contrast, Jesus Christ offers salvation to those who join His righteous kingdom of Heaven, love others more than themselves, and love and obey God above all else. Why not use Jesus Christ our King's own definition of salvation instead of using worldly Christianity's definition?

What do we mean by total surrender to God? What do we think He is going to call us to? Send us to some unreached jungle tribe? Call us to be an Air Force pilot in a foreign combat zone? Sometimes I think our expression of "total surrender to God" is better defined as an introverted infatuation with our own deceitful hearts. The correct New Testament holy living definition of "total surrender to God" is obedience to Jesus' teachings and integration with a holy brotherhood. Total obedience to Jesus' teachings and surrender to a holy brotherhood has the power to change the way we interact with *ourselves*. The pattern of God speaking through other people has been the standard God-method for thousands of years. Why should some starry-eyed holy roller convince us otherwise? If you are too spiritual to submit to a Christian brotherhood, how do you expect to fit into Heaven?

Are we mistaking personal devotions for personal devotion? God wants a relationship with us but that relationship is not measured by our knowledge of scripture, by our personal testimony, or by how we claim to feel about God. It is not measured by how long our prayers are or by our daily scripture reading. It is measured by our relationship to our fellow man. If we cannot get along with people who we can see, how can we claim to love a God who we cannot see?[2]

I understand there are times when a person needs to make a change to a different church group. And that may include a period of time that leaves us with no clear commitment to any church group. But the attitude that Christianity is just "me and my sweet Jesus" is from Satan. *An overemphasis on personal salvation has led to an epidemic of this type of thinking.* We are a part of Christ if we are a part of His body, "members one of another." It is time to take a careful look at corporate salvation. "Do you not know that a little leaven leavens the whole lump?"[3]

Do not take this to mean you do not need to be born again. The new birth and baptism are essentials of the faith. But worldly Christianity has taken almost all

---

[2] 1 John 4:20.

[3] 1 Cor. 5:6.

meaning away from the terms "saved" or "born again." This terminology is almost useless in determining someone's relationship with Jesus.

Worldly Christianity has offered us a relationship with Jesus in exchange for our Christian culture; *it has delivered neither.*

CHAPTER 3
Twice the Son of Hell

The unrighteous will not inherit the kingdom of God.[1]

The gospel is racing naked around the world, stripped of its weapons and its real meaning. Worldly evangelists are spreading their American, militant, immoral, immodest, individualistic, "save me," culturally relevant, humanistic, stripped down "gospel" to millions of unfortunate souls around the globe. The people saved by this fatally simplified gospel are—surprise, surprise—militant, immoral, immodest, individualistic, "save me," culturally relevant, and humanistic. Why are we drawn to join in the shameless spectacle that they call evangelism? The model is perverted. What is exciting about the tearful testimonies that this

---

[1] 1 Cor. 6:9.

prostituted "gospel" elicits? Why should we be inspired when they spout numbers of how many people they have deceived and inoculated against the real gospel and its accompanying good works?

Instead of groveling in shoe licking admiration at these great missionaries we should be sickened by the unimaginable horror of it all. *Millions of souls think they have a free pass to Heaven.* The "save me gospel" of personal salvation is not the Good News of the kingdom. This diluted "gospel" does not save people from a burning hell, it merely comforts them on their way to hell. God forbid that we be party to this diabolic carnage. The Revelation of Jesus Christ describes a place prepared for those who make and love a lie.

In contrast New Testament holy living calls for investing in relational discipleship (one who copies his teacher) and brotherhood accountability as the inseparable vehicle of the gospel.[2] Delivery is slow, painful and anything but efficient. And lives are truly changed. The gospel is not American; it predates and transcends time and place. The gospel is not militant; it extends peace, love, and nonviolence to all men. The gospel is not immoral; it calls us to "not even a hint" of sexual immorality.[3] The gospel is not immodest; good works are our fashion statements. The gospel is not individualistic; it is corporate. The gospel is not "save

---

[2] Luke 6:40.

[3] Eph. 5:3.

me;" it is the Good News of a righteous King redeeming a nation for Himself. The gospel is not culturally relevant; it is a holy counter culture. The gospel is not humanistic; it is about God and His glory.

The gospel is an invitation to join this righteous nation (the church) and become a part of God's people. The gospel invites us to deny ourselves for the good of the greater body.

Introducing converts to New Testament holy living is *hard* work. It is not simply saying a quick prayer. Instead, it is to engage in the life changing work of joining, submitting to, and caring for the bride of Christ. It is to reject the error of Hezekiah, who was content to have peace in his lifetime. We need to have a multigenerational corporate vision to provide stable Christian communities. *It is not just about us and our relationship with Jesus; instead, it is about kingdom communities that embody the Good News.* Results are measured in generations, not in minutes or hours.

If suicide was approved as an exit strategy, many worldly Christians would already be gone. With the gospel stripped of its meaning and power, the only thing left to offer is a free trip to Heaven. Personal pleasure is the ultimate goal. The precious heavenly reward of the saints has become an end in itself. *How tragic!*

VISION CASTING

CHAPTER 4
Begin with the End in Mind

If you aim at nothing, you will hit it every time.[1]

Think about what you wish the church to look like in one hundred years. Short-term visions lead to foolish compromises. In the now famous words of Steven Covey, *"Begin with the end in mind."*[2]

As Christians we all can relate to living with the end in mind. We believe that how we live our lives directly impacts how we will spend eternity. As humans we believe that how we spend our money affects our bank accounts. We believe that how we farm impacts our yields. Most of us believe that how we dress affects our relationship with God. But curiously, we have

---

[1] Zig Ziglar.

[2] Steven Covey, *The Seven Habits of Highly Effective People* (New York: Simon & Schuster, 2020), Habit 2.

decided to be mostly unintentional about how we direct church growth. We have silently chewed our cud, built good walls and long lanes, and been content to split haphazardly over minutia. We build strong churches in the shadow of other strong churches. On a given Sunday morning we drive past brothers and sisters of every stripe and color to worship in our perfectly curated unified fellowship of believers. We have worshiped at the altar of uniformity and developed curious obsessions with head-covering patterns. And when someone offends us, or some unspiritual sister in our midst rounds the corners of her covering a little too much, we drive off to another more perfect church in the area without ever having to leave the comfort of our familiar acreage.

Maybe you fear the downward spiral of intentionalism. One well-meaning brother even went so far as to write a paper about the dangers of intentionalism. We can be driven by the irrational fear of choosing a direction and be swept along in the current of lethargy and fatalism that characterizes too many of our churches. Maybe we occasionally gasp a few gulps of revivalism. We can dance around the fire of revivalism like bloodthirsty savages and hope to "reclaim" some imagined spiritual utopia of the past, or we can choose to be proactive in our choices.

The purpose of this book is to *promote intentional church division.* Let's think about how to do that well.

I challenge you to spend some time thinking deeply about the church one hundred years from now. You will be gone. Your disciples will live on. Will you have passed on the faith? Have you equipped your children to pass on the faith? Did our churches add to our numbers daily? Have we been so focused on evangelism that we assimilated into the world? Or have we so selfishly clung to our lifestyle that no outsiders were allowed in, and thus embalmed our culture and condemned our physical offspring to a plethora of genetic defects?

As you think about the church in one hundred years, remember that you will not get there alone. *Individual idealism works against corporate progress.* You are not good enough to carry the church forward alone.

Chapter 5
Change Your Mind About Missions

The eyes of a fool are on the ends of the earth.[1]

Think "local church" rather than "foreign mission." Worldly missiology has ravaged churches on all sides of the globe. Churches begin to think that souls are always hidden in some unreached corner or forbidden culture. People barely fit to be local church members are filling prominent roles in foreign missions. Boards and budgets have replaced bread and porches as the preferred tools of evangelism. We feel guilty if we spend unscheduled time with people because we are not following the latest six-step evangelism fad.

I have a dream: what if we stopped fantasizing about short-term missions and began relentlessly

---

[1] Pro. 17:24.

placing churches in strategic locations. And I am not talking about perfect neighborhood assault plans. Instead, place plain communities where there are not already plain communities. This *super simple strategy alone* could have an Anabaptist church on the doorstep of almost the entire United States population in a few short years. We have the resources to put a living gospel witness in front of most Americans very quickly, but *we lack the will.*

We find it easier to read glamorous missionary stories and good books on how to do missions. Our stagnant churches resort to worldly evangelism tactics. Some believe they need to destroy their church culture to make it more palatable to the unchurched. Some of us begin to evangelize like we have a limited hunting season and a certain amount of deer tags to fill. Some people who are suffering from an evangelistic works guilt complex feel compelled to speak to every person they meet about their soul. This guilt complex can hijack meaningful personal connections, and leave those we are trying to reach feeling hunted, judged and alienated.

Many evangelism methods take a ton of work and energy away from our other responsibilities. Often mission programs try to exploit the power of relationships in their evangelism programs. But real relationships cannot be rushed or faked. Potential converts quickly feel used and become bitter when what they thought was a friendship becomes a religious sales pitch. Converts are puzzled when friendships that they hoped could blossom and deepen vaporize and go sour after they join the church.

Historically, many people have come to the Anabaptist churches because a family or an individual took a genuine interest in them. Keep that relationship genuine. People are seeking authenticity, not cultural relevance.

In the early church, many converts had their own sponsors.[2] A brother or sister would befriend some individual. If and when that person developed an interest in the Christian faith their friend would help them decide if they were ready to join the church. When the time was right the Christian friend would bring them to the church elders as a sponsor. The sponsor might attend instructive meetings with the new convert. The sponsor would be responsible to make sure the convert was living above sin. They may play the role of mediator in misunderstandings between the convert and church members. This was not a "say-a-little-prayer-and-pour-a-little-water" type of church membership. Individual church members played a huge role in discipling new believers. This relationship was not a casual one but rather a very long-term commitment on the part of the sponsor. The process of joining the church took quite some time in

---

[2] Alan Kreider, *The Patient Ferment of the Early Church* (Grand Rapids, MI: Baker Academic, 2016), 149.

that era, sometimes up to five years. Sponsors may have continued in a mentoring role far beyond that, probably for life. Could we learn from them?

What if we cast off our chains of worldly American missiology? What if we unashamedly rejected the false worldly evangelism teaching creeping into our churches? There is extreme pressure on churches to lower our ethics to accommodate seekers. Has that ever worked? Could we learn from history? What if we went to our Amish brothers for clues about church expansion? What if we insisted on adhering to the faith once delivered?[3] What if everyone took an active role in discipling newcomers? And what if we prioritized the disciples in our own houses and neighborhoods?

These two simple methods could lead to explosive church growth. Start new churches in new places, and disciple our own households and neighborhoods. *We would not have time for worldly evangelism programs.*

---

[3] Jude 1:3.

Chapter 6
Simple Math

Figures don't lie but liars can figure.

The interesting thing about math is that it is a hard science. Numbers are hard to argue with. If we look at the groups that have fairly closely followed the teachings of Jesus, it is easy to see who has been most prolific. I can see the excuses and protests popping into your minds, but let's take a moment to honestly assess.

Most worldly churches are not making disciples in their own households. Their diluted religion is not even attractive to their own offspring. This is not just my biased assumption; it is a documented area of concern for many churches. Yet many of these worldly Christians are very active in missions and church life. They feel good about saving many souls even as the few in their households are lost. It is a common thread among worldly missionaries to question the wisdom of burdening ourselves with too many children in light of all the souls to be reached. Worldly American Christianity is losing momentum in the United States.

Now let's think about the Amish. They adhere to most of the teachings of Jesus. No divorce, no openly immoral relationships, financial community, no oaths, no lawsuits, no killing. But all these good things are completely dismissed on two accounts. Number one, Amish trust in works for their salvation. Number two, Amish are not evangelistic.

Hopefully if you have read this far you are beginning to understand that point number one is irrelevant. This is a trumped-up allegation based on a flawed understanding of salvation and a few bad actors. It can be mostly dismissed.

The second allegation is more complex. Amish definitely do not approach evangelism from the same angle as worldly Christianity does. Integration of converts into Amish culture is pretty rare. Some Amish churches are changing this, but overall, you are unlikely to encounter an Amish person who was not raised Amish. So how is the Amish population expanding so rapidly?

The Amish population doubles about every twenty years. Even with the current lower than historical average family size of five to seven children, an almost 85% retention rate is creating exponential population growth. And these two factors are key. With a 100% retention rate and an average family size of two children a population would slowly shrink. Most liberal Mennonites that are trying to be more evangelistic have a much lower average family size combined with a fairly low retention rate.

    Let's look at the retention rate first. Amish children know who they are. They do not confuse themselves with Protestants or Catholics. They have a clear choice between being Amish or worldly. As a culture becomes less clear about who they are, and who they are not, it becomes much easier to assimilate into surrounding culture. When anyone who names the name of Christ becomes our inner circle, we lose our identity. This becomes increasingly true as we begin to adopt worldly Christianity's definition of salvation and methods of evangelism.

    Now how about family size? I repeatedly hear the argument that Amish growth is only through procreation. Honestly, I am rather weary of that argument. It just points to their incredibly successful teaching program. A Christian culture that cares for their elderly, their children, their young mothers, and their sick is nothing to be snuffed at. Plus, they honor the sanctity of marriage, make provisions for their youth to acquire life partners, structure their social lives around child care and family life, provide business opportunities for young men, and teach gender appropriate work skills to children. Contrast this to a worldly Christian society that promotes child-free marriages, delayed marriages, nursing homes for the elderly, confusion of gender roles, and detachment from business under the guise of being free for the Lord's work.

Should the Amish be more evangelistic? Of course. I think a little outward vision could be beautiful. But they should not sacrifice a godly culture and high retention rate to gain the approval of apostate missionaries and world facing Mennonites. And neither should you and I. We must balance discipling our own and our outreach or we will simply become more swindlers casting our pearls to the swine.

God is smarter than we are. His patterns are for our good. He said children are good; it is time for us to stop arguing with Him. Have children and disciple them. Why is it glitzier to witness than to change diapers or to teach school? Who says children inhibit ministry? Are children not humans? Do they not have souls? Have we bought into worldly missions' liberal political myth of overpopulation? It is time for us to embrace church growth through procreation. Let God be true and every man a liar.[1]

Totally embracing our calling as a multigenerational church includes creating employment opportunities, life companion opportunities, housing opportunities, church leadership opportunities, and risk opportunities. We

---

[1] Rom. 3:4.

need to think about ways to help young people thrive. We need to find ways to help people explore their potential.

    Make a new church. Make a few converts in each church. Develop enough resources to care for each disciple fully. Make lots of disciples in your own households. Focus on retention. This is huge. Worldly Christianity is not doing this. If we are able to maintain fertility and retention rates while simultaneously bringing in a few converts our churches will thrive.

    Rinse and repeat. That the whole world may know.

CHAPTER 7
Look What Worked

The proof of the pudding is in the eating.

A Moravian missionary visited our Mennonite ancestors in the 1740s. He was disappointed that they seemed to be taken up in making a living and were not interested in his message. I believe he was actually observing a key difference between the Mennonites and the Moravians. The Moravians came to evangelize the natives, they did not appear overly concerned with the material world, they promoted extreme discipline, community of goods, and deemphasized family ties. God has set up His church with a multitude of gifts. The Moravians heavily emphasized the few gifts that they thought were more spiritual. They put extra weight on community, corporate and personal spiritual activity, and discipline.

But sadly, the Moravians that exist today would be unrecognizable to their ancestors.

The Mennonites came as settlers, they wanted a place to bring up their families in peace and the fear of God. They also believed in living holy lives. But they believed families were essential, even central to the church. They believed in working with their hands. Their faith in God was less focused on spiritual activity and verbal testimony. The Mennonites concentrated more on obedience to God and preserving a Christian culture. They mostly rejected elaborate theologies in favor of quietly living holy lives. Their more pietistic brothers falsely assumed that Anabaptists were not interested in spiritual things. But I suspect the Mennonites would have been pretty interested in less abstract spiritual discussions. In fact, there are many records of their dependence upon the provision of God, of their refusal to swear oaths, of their willingness to suffer rather than defend themselves in any manner, of their faithfulness to their families, and of their mercy towards the Native Americans. Many Mennonites today differ very little from the faith and practice of their ancestors.

The dilemma we face today is how to evangelize better than our ancestors without falling into the same trap as the many others who have walked this path before. The saddest thing about history is how often we fail to learn from it. If we do not honestly assess the mistakes of our forefathers, we will likely be doomed to repeat them. Nearly every group tends towards preserving culture at the expense of evangelism or promoting evangelism at the expense of culture.

Let's briefly explore the idea of preserving culture at the expense of evangelism. The Amish are the best strawmen for this example. Many people think the Amish do not evangelize at all. They spend much effort preserving and promoting a culture that will provide a God-fearing heritage for their own children. They so strongly believe in being separate from the world that they take extra steps to prevent the world from influencing their families. They speak German in church services to build a bigger barrier between them and the world. And this has been effective. In many ways they have brought the kingdom of God to earth. But in fixating on a Christian culture, they have built a barrier that few can cross, whether coming or going.

The other strawman is evangelical Christianity. Because they believe that salvation is mostly about verbal testimonies and mental assent, they fixate on evangelism with almost no interest in real Christian culture. After all, works do not save you. Their failure to allow a Christian culture and their emphasis on *sola fide* enables an environment of lawlessness. It has been documented that the more people in an area claim faith in Jesus, the higher the crime rates are.[1] How does that relate to the power of the Holy Spirit in worldly Christians' lives? Yet many Anabaptist people are gravitating toward this foolish fixation on evangelism. How many times does it have to not work until we are convinced that it will not work? The gospel separated from the Good News of the kingdom is dead faith.

One of the ironies of this dichotomy is that the "non evangelistic" Amish are world famous for their Christian culture. They have inspired many others to live holy lives, even if these people did not directly join them. People come from all over the world to visit Amish country. The Amish have somewhat accidentally become a city on a hill.

So how does all this apply to us? First, we must value Christian culture. The Bible prescribes faith and works. Not a faith that works, not a working faith, not a deep love of Jesus that makes us long to obey Him. Faith and works. Faith and works need to be accepted on equal footing. And we all tend toward one or the other. This is where we must recognize and value diversity of gifts. Some brothers will be more evangelistic, some will care more about building Christian culture. But we must never diminish holy

---

[1] Tyler O'Neil, "Bible Belt Has Most Sinners, Research Suggests: How Sinful is Your State?", The Christian Post, December 20, 2013, https://www.christianpost.com/news/bible-belt-has-most-sinners-research-suggests-how-sinful-is-your-state.html.

Christian living to make our evangelism more effective. Noah preached for many years with no souls saved except his family. Effectiveness is not a useful measuring device *by itself*.

I suggest we look for ways to present a Christian culture to more people. This can be done by any group that is presenting the gospel in their daily lives. There is no need for 501(c)(3)s, mission organizations, fancy evangelism programs, or children's ministries. We just need people who care about living holy lives and are willing to serve others. We should not need artificial barriers to keep out the world. And we should not need artificially low barriers to bring souls into the kingdom. Separation from the world is a natural result of becoming a true disciple of Jesus.

The easiest (and hardest) way to present the gospel to people is to go live with them. Be careful about evangelism methods that try to circumvent living our lives with the people we hope to reach. Short circuiting a godly multigenerational New Testament culture with the excuse that we are fulfilling the great commission is futile. The proper way to fulfill the great commission is to get off our piles and spread across the country. Our faithful heritage was no accident. The only effective way to evangelize and preserve godly culture is to take the culture with us as we settle into new places.

Become settlers. Become a student of history. Do not be content to merely preserve a museum quality gospel. Leave the Tower of Babel and become a city on a hill.[2]

Invade new territory and "Occupy until I come."[3]

---

[2] Matt. 5:14.

[3] Luke 19:13.

COMFORT CRISIS

CHAPTER 8
Comfort Mindset

*Because you are lukewarm [. . .]
I will vomit you out of My mouth.*[1]

Decadence. By dividing our lives into spiritual activity and non-spiritual activity we have accidentally removed whole life accountability. Now we can live lives of carnal decadence while being in good standing with the church. We bask in leather, luxury, expansive yards, fine furniture, beautiful houses, shiny cars, dripping desserts and polished shoes. We are far removed from donkeys, sweat, dust and sandals. And it shows.

We are addicted to structure and security. We love being surrounded by extended family. We love the comfort of familiar places. We make rules in the name

---

[1] Rev. 3:16.

of uniformity that are mostly just to protect us from messy people. We like our little rhythms and socials. Sometimes we feel guilty about our lack of spiritual fervor. So, we ratchet up the spiritual noise without dealing with the real issue. We do not even realize this. We inherit unrealistic expectations of revival. Bible studies, church services and revival meetings will not fix this. *The real problem is within us.*

What if we invited some foreigners to our next grill out? What if we kicked our addiction to structure and security? What if we started caring about people: white people, rich people, poor people, black people, Mexican people, Iraqi people, and the foreigners living among you? What if we stopped overthinking unity? Would the church grow? Could we become more unified around our purpose of church building instead of creating false symbols of unity? Could we come out of our sanitized little world and actually sit with people where they are? Way too many plain people drip elitist and racist attitudes as they defend their self-indulgent lifestyles. That is not Jesus, and it should not be His body.

Large, well-structured churches allow the majority of the members to live in comfort. And we love it. We love the firewalls protecting us from the world. We have cleverly disguised rules designed to protect our comfort, and we pretend they are necessary to protect us from the world. We have created a special bureaucracy designed to absolve all parties of personal responsibility. We choose leaders that can beat up our enemies instead of choosing leaders that are Christlike shepherds. When a situation calls for discernment or mercy we respond in judgment, shrug and say, "We know it's not right but that's what the church requires." Then we wipe our mouths, go back to our grills, prayer meetings, and choir practice like nothing ever happened. We like our comfortable little religion and are willing to destroy anyone who threatens to make it messy.

In our culture of comfort, we have become very efficient at reducing inconvenience. This is not wrong in itself. But we humans are always trying to move to the next level. As we become more efficient, we have more time and money for leisure. We begin to use this leisure time for pleasure seeking. Soon small pleasures become normal and we begin seeking bigger, more expensive pleasures. Backyard spikeball is replaced by golf. Hunting and fishing for meat with the family is replaced by sporting trips, fishing tournaments and safaris. Eating out a couple times a year is replaced by frequent trips to nice restaurants. Trips to visit family and church friends are replaced by yearly trips to Europe. Some of this is not wrong in itself, but what happens next?

As we become conditioned to more and more comfort, convenience, and pleasure, we become less tolerant of discomfort, inconvenience, and suffering. And if we are serious about starting new churches in new areas, *we are going to need to get comfortable being uncomfortable.* We will have less leisure. We will have less money. We will not be with our old friends. We will not be with our extended families. We will need to make new relationships. We will need to relate well with difficult people. We may need to miss family reunions. In other words, our lives will lose the neat little edges we love so well. We will not be able to indulge our flesh in every pleasure and comfort that our hearts desire. And that is a good thing. It is arguably one of the bigger benefits of intentional church division.

This is war. We need hardened soldiers who are willing to sacrifice comforts for the kingdom. We need soldiers who are willing to occupy new territories. Misguided asceticism has long been a plague of the church. Religious radicals have recognized the lethal epidemic of comfort seeking but they address it in the wrong way. In an expansion-focused church, there is plenty of pain to go around. There is no need to create silly programs and practices aimed at crucifying the flesh.

Embrace the pain, crucify the flesh, expand the kingdom. Fight like men. Softies need not apply.

Chapter 9
Consumer Churches

The people sat down to eat and drink, and rose up to play.[1]

Is your church house comfortable? Do you have enough room? Do you have room for visitors? Do you have climate control? Do you have a nursery? Do you have a kitchen? Do you have a place to eat, like a dining hall? Do you have a pulpit? Do you have a recording system? Do you have padded seating? Is there a part of your church building you call the sanctuary? Do you have indoor restrooms? Do you have Sunday School rooms? Did you know that none of this is necessary to have a church?

How about your church services? Do you dress up in your Sunday best? Do you shine your shoes and your car (or buggy) for church? Would you be

---

[1] 1 Cor. 10:7.

uncomfortable if someone showed up in clean work clothes? Would a car with rust, dirt, or dents be out of place in your church parking lot? Does it bother you if noisy children disturb the services? Are there too many children in your service? Is your idea of worship based on silence, comfort, and ritual? Does it bother you when the singing is off tune? Do you expect a sermon? Are there a few ordained brothers expected to preach each Sunday? Would anyone notice if you did not show up to a Sunday service? Do you have one or more responsibilities that you would need to have someone else cover if you were not going to be at a Sunday service?

Should the Sunday service be a time to relax and unwind, a social showcase of the clean and shiny side of us?

Many of us would be extremely uncomfortable in a house church. We do not want to get that close to our religion. We do not want people running around in our houses. In a close group we cannot hide behind our nicely pressed suit and our witty Sunday School remarks. People begin to see us for who we really are. We cannot sit back and rely on groupthink. We feel self-conscious. We would rather drive to a big church an hour away to hide among the crowds and feel good.

Imagine how you would react to the church service conditions described in Acts: a crowded upstairs room, seating and ventilation that evidently was not great (considering some poor fellow was sitting in the window).² Because many people were slaves (and therefore not free to assemble with the church until the day's duties were done), evening services were common in this era. Would you feel reverent sitting in someone's upstairs apartment, packed with sweaty bodies, bugs buzzing around, standing or sitting on the floor, no indoor plumbing, bad lighting, and no fans or air conditioning? Many foreign missionaries accept these types of conditions as normal. But as soon as we return home, they are unacceptable, irreverent, and repulsive. We think we need church houses in order to validate our notion of church. *But church houses are a part of the problem.*

As the church began to lose its life and became more structured, church houses became the default position. Power hungry church and government leaders welcomed this shift as it gave them more control over the group. No longer did small groups meet in each other's homes and in public places, instead in many places rules were created to forbid meeting outside a church building. These church buildings quickly became extravagant. Critics of the church often question the need for this opulence. And rightly so. Our Anabaptist forefathers held various opinions on this matter. Some were very opposed to church buildings. Today many of the plain churches that allow church buildings require that they be simple, without

---

² Acts 20:9.

JESUS AND THE MENNONITES

steeples or stained glass. But one group, the Amish, have forbidden church houses entirely.

The Amish are one of the largest and fastest growing plain churches. We discuss some of the reasons for their growth in Chapter 6, but here I want to consider their rejection of church buildings. I believe this is a helpful case study of church building ownership. If you look back at the description of the church services in Acts, they could almost describe a modern Amish service. Obviously, some key components are missing among the Amish, such as the Lord's Supper each Sunday, prophecy, prayer, and the apostle Paul. But their lack of church houses, combined with a decentralized church government, has given them a significant church expansion advantage. Let's think about the reason.

If the Amish want to start a new church they move to a new locality. It is uncommon for Amish to start a new church brand in the same area. Gradually over many years, new Amish brands have developed. But nowhere near the level of their centralized, building-based Anabaptist counterparts. Part of the reason is that the Amish tend to see the local church as geographically united. If a church gets too large, they divide along geographic lines, creating a new district. If a brother wants to move to a new area, he is free to do so. If other families join him, it becomes a new district. Usually, a minister will eventually move in, or in the rare cases that a minister does not move in one is ordained. This method is a drastic simplification of church expansion. There is no need for bureaucracy, committees, church policies, buildings, real estate, endless meetings, financial oversight, voting, or planning. That makes it really simple. Amish districts are popping up all over rural America. Severing our attachment to church houses is a step in the right direction.

Once we move away from our church building addiction maybe some of our other addictions will loosen their stranglehold. Maybe our services would become less of an embalmed ritual or a shiny shoe show, less comfortable and less fake, and would instead become more participatory, more relevant, more intense, more vibrant, more messy, and more real. They could also become a lot more portable. And that is the point.

God's people have always struggled with an adulterous relationship to structure and structures. From the Tower of Babel to the golden calves to Solomon's temple to the Mennonite General Conference, the temptation to become sedentary and dependent upon man has been irresistible. We need to repent of the adulterous dependency on church buildings and bureaucracies. Grind up the golden calves, drink the golden water, and pick up your swords. It is time for churches to start investing in developing people, not real estate.

JESUS AND THE MENNONITES

God is calling us back to mobility and a reliance on Him. He wants us to leave all and follow His lead. *It will never be comfortable. This mobile dependence upon God is key to kingdom expansion.*

CHAPTER 10
Risk Aversion

They immediately left their nets and followed Him.[1]

There is a short story in the Bible about a man who fought a lion in a pit on a snowy day.[2] We plain people have definitely lost that vision; we are more like the lazy man in Proverbs who refuses to go out because there is a lion in the street.[3] We accept mediocrity rather than embrace change. We are risk averse.

Challenges help us feel alive. It is no accident that suicide rates are highest in wealthy societies. No one wants to just exist. Entrenching in our good traditions may seem like a great way to preserve our

---

[1] Matt. 4:20.

[2] 1 Chron. 11:22.

[3] Pro. 26:13.

youth. But most churches fail to give their youth any opportunity to make a truly useful contribution. Our bright eyed and sincere youth are drawn to the galvanizing stories of missionaries. They wistfully dream of ways they could make a useful contribution on the mission fields. There is no shortage of books about the powerful struggles and rewards of missionary life. In their zeal to be useful to God they fail to see the insidious spider web of false doctrines that often accompany these heart tugging stories.

Jesus repeatedly invites us to risk all for the kingdom. Yet in modern American Anabaptism we have done everything in our power to mitigate risk. The young lion fighters in our midst are regulated to wrangling tame house cats in a sterile arena. *We are protected from every enemy except ourselves.* And thus, the Christian life earns its perception as a boring, emasculated, sterile ritual best suited for little old ladies and funeral homes. Because we are uncomfortable with too much passion, young people, especially young men, are sent to the mission fields to work off some of their zeal. Christians become nothing more than bored hypocrites trying to put on a joyful show for the Lord. Spiritual activity is overemphasized. Men begin to seek meaning in business and play while women seek meaning in social status. And the church loses its power and appeal.

How could we become more comfortable with risk? Increased responsibility brings life and meaning to our lives. It also increases our risk. But we are not created to be carefree and tended. Children begin seeking adventure early in their lives. Young men long for the opportunity for conquest. As humans we crave responsibility and meaning. We quickly become depressed and hopeless when we do not perceive ourselves as being useful. Very small children can quickly see through jobs that are created only to keep them occupied. And our youth also recognize very quickly when they are not needed in the church. Outside of marriage and child bearing many larger groups do not have any good ways for young people to actually be useful. So what is the solution?

The solution is smaller groups. A smaller group actually needs everyone. Many times, there are not enough people to go around. Less experienced and less capable people have to shoulder bigger loads. And this is risky. Things can go wrong in this environment. And that is good. We learn by doing. We become better at things much faster by doing them. A diversity of talents is developed fairly rapidly. These newfound talents can then be further developed and a flywheel of risk taking and responsibility is set in motion. As everyone becomes more comfortable with risk and responsibility, we open ourselves to more risk and responsibility. The goal is that everyone is meaningfully engaged and equipped. The next step is church expansion.

These equipped and responsible people of all ages are now prepared to take on new territory. It is definitely not without risks. But it is worth ditching the stagnant, default, no-risk model for a powerful, risky, New Testament model. We no longer need all kinds of programs and ministries to entertain our young energy. The horizon is open for conquest. They can do real work. They are now equipped to start new churches in new areas.

It will take a lot of effort to break our old habits of risk aversion. But it can be done, and must be done if we are going to create an environment where young people can thrive. As we break this pattern of stagnation and begin to shoulder our way out into new environments, there will be much to learn and plenty for everyone to do. *The church will regain the gleam in her eyes, and nations will see the energy and power of the house of the Lord.* And the nations will say "Come, and let us go up to the mountain of the Lord."[4]

Saul was taking it easy under the pomegranate tree in Gibeah. But Jonathan said to the young armor bearer at his side, "Come, let us go over to the Philistines, maybe God will work for us. *God is not limited by the size of the army.*" So, Jonathan said to his armor bearer, "Climb up after me; the Lord has given them into the hand of Israel."[5]

---

[4] Isa. 2:3.

[5] 1 Sam. 14:6–12, paraphrase.

Chapter 11
Opportunity Cost

Is there something I want much more than this?

What is this mediocrity costing us? What else could we do with our resources? Every resource we steward is finite. Our time is finite. Our money is finite. Our health is finite. Our family is finite. Our church is finite. Our knowledge is finite. Our skills are finite. Our relationships are finite. Our food is finite. What does this mean?

This means that if I spend my time, my health, my skills, and my knowledge on professional football I cannot use that time, health, skills, or knowledge on church expansion. If I spend my twenties touring Europe, I cannot invest that time raising a family. If I spend profits from my business on a vacation home, I cannot invest that money providing a young father with a better paying job. If a church goes into debt to build a new meeting place, they cannot use those resources for planting a new church. If I burn out my family in pursuit of a career, farm, or business, I do not allow them to be used in building up the church. If I need dinner invitations that only include those whom I am comfortable with, I cannot use those mealtimes to bless strangers. If I spend my reading time reading romance novels, I cannot use that time to read Anabaptist history. If I spend my time accumulating knowledge about auto racing, I cannot use that time to accumulate knowledge about growing tomatoes. If I focus my energy on making my life as comfortable as possible, I cannot use that energy to improve a low-class neighborhood. If I invest money in a retirement fund, that money is no longer available to the kingdom.

The list of opportunity costs is endless. If we begin to think like investors, we will slowly begin to change the way we live our lives. Many worldly investors deny themselves passing pleasures. They prefer to invest five dollars rather than spend it on a sugary drink at Starbucks. They often drive their vehicles longer than other people because they have counted the cost of a newer vehicle and do not want to waste money that could otherwise be invested.

So, think about opportunity cost and investment opportunity. *What if the next time we make a decision as a church we would think, "Could we do something better?"* Should we send one family to Africa for two years, or could we send five families to Chicago to start a new church? Should we expand our auditorium, or should we send ten families to rural Louisiana? Should we go pass out tracts or should we invite a lonely neighbor over to lunch? Should I go elk hunting in Wyoming or should I visit that little church in Alaska? Should I wash my car for Sunday or should I help a young mother clean her house?

I am not advocating depriving ourselves of every earthly pleasure. I am suggesting that when we have an opportunity to participate in a pleasurable activity we weigh it thoughtfully, rather than greedily scooping up every opportunity to indulge ourselves. We have developed a well-oiled godly culture and are at a place to harvest much good. We can continue to raise the bar on selfish consumption or we can choose to funnel our time, energy, money, health, knowledge, culture, families, farms, and churches to expand the kingdom.

I do not know about you, but I want more, a whole lot more. I cannot keep from thinking about ways to expand the church. I drive through areas and think, "Wow! We could start a new church here." Starting a new church could make more logistical sense than sending one family to China for a year. It would definitely be a lot more rewarding than nursing a fifty-year-old territorial feud with that neighboring congregation.

I want more. Much more. I hope you do, too.

STRATEGIES FOR CONQUEST

CHAPTER 12
Empower Your People

The person who grabs the cat by the tail learns about forty percent faster than the one just watching.[1]

This chapter is especially for leaders. I'm not using a narrow definition of leader here. If anyone is following you it makes you a leader. Often leaders get consumed with putting out daily fires. We are so focused on problem solving that we forget to create learning opportunities. Look around you. Do you see young men and women who could be developed for future church expansion? Can you create opportunities for them to learn by doing?

Let's think about the skills needed to start new churches. We need people who can teach the Word. We need people who can cook. We need people with

---

[1] Mark Twain.

construction skills. We need people who can lead singing. We need people who are skilled in hospitality. We need people who are flexible. We need people who can do paperwork. We need people who are familiar with fasting. We need people who know how to run a business. We need people who can pray. We need people who can teach school. We need people who can manage money well. We need people who can relate well to others. We need people who have backbone. We need people who can babysit. We need people who can sit by the fire and listen. We need peacemakers, we really need peacemakers. And so much more.

  Often, we direct all our efforts to developing the next ministers, elders, deacons, or bishops. There is so much more to leadership. Develop leadership skills. Develop thinking skills. Develop with intention to send out. Focusing on helping everyone become leaders in their own realm is more valuable than grooming several individuals for limited leadership roles.

  Ladies' roles in leadership are often misunderstood. They either think men are the leaders and thus they are off the hook or they feel like they have to be leading Bible study classes with other women to actually be leaders. But the reality is much more subtle than this. Sisters' circle of influence is greater than most of us realize. We need faithful sisters who care for their families, bless the poor, know how to dress modestly, care for the aged, know how to prepare a meal, can control their appetite, can control their tongues, can host company, can cultivate a garden, know how to care for the sick, know how to make do with less, can keep a clean house, and so much more.

But this does not happen by accident. It takes a culture of faithful women to teach girls and young women these skills. The older women teaching the younger women is the biblical pattern. Paul's list of qualities of women says nothing about leading Bible studies.[2] While there are occasional needs for sisters to teach, it should mostly be one on one. It appears that women were a primary driver in the spread of the gospel in the first century.[3]

Most women have the gift of communication. When the believing wife of an unbelieving merchant moved to another town, the wife would spread the good news among her new friends. A woman's influence on and support of her husband are seriously underestimated. Many men in the first century were probably introduced to Christianity through their wife or slave women.[4] Many young men have been drawn back to the narrow way by the intercessory prayers of their mothers. The living example of a believing woman is a powerful and beautiful testimony.

An illuminating thought on a sister's role in leadership: If you think women are not leaders, just

---

[2] Titus 2:3–5.

[3] *The Patient Ferment of the Early Church*, 82.

[4] *The Patient Ferment of the Early Church*, chap. 4.

look at how quickly a new dress pattern or house decor theme spreads through your community.

So please do not buy into worldly Christianity's narrative that mocks homemakers as barefoot and pregnant while lifting up women "missionaries" and spiritual leaders. *Every culture that has bought into this narrative has quickly descended into chaos and wickedness.* Even as early as the writing of Revelation 2, Jesus warns the church about allowing a woman, under the guise of prophecy, to teach. Make no apologies for obedience to the pattern of gender roles set in place by the Head of the church.

But do not fall into the other ditch of denigrating the value of women in the work of the church. Women fill valuable roles in homemaking and ministering to women and children that men cannot or should not fill. Girls need to understand that a woman's calling in the church is not inferior to a man's but different. The church has traditionally recognized single or widowed women as powerful private prayer warriors. It is the responsibility of church leaders to defend, protect, and elevate the correct role of sisters in the church.

So, push those young people. Put work that matters in front of them quickly. Have young girls learn to babysit responsibly. Teach them to cook wholesome meals. Have them learn at a young age how to manage a household well. Much of the physical health in a congregation is determined by the homemakers. Have young men learn to participate in physical labor. Engage youth of both genders in conversations about the future of the church. Teach them to pray. Warn them about false doctrines. *Create safe places for them to fail.* Give them opportunities to lead others under your guidance. So many of the factors that determine a church's ability to thrive are overlooked by leaders who focus only on the spiritual.

Maybe your church has been sheltered and there are older people who need encouragement to try new things. Give them the space to do that. Sometimes families who are unfamiliar with a Christian culture join the church. Many times these people have overdeveloped spiritual gifts but no understanding of Christian culture. You will need to gently develop their understanding of embodied gospel.

Leaders, do not be too defensive of your position. Develop others more capable than yourselves. Make church expansion your passion. Think beyond yourself. Think beyond protecting your little corner. Cast the vision for starting churches in new places. Enable those who catch the vision. Rarely will these people be properly equipped for the work. Find the right people to go with them. Be willing to go. Be willing to send. Be willing to bless those who do it differently than how you think is best. You are not indispensable. Satan loves to use men's egos to stifle the spread of the church.

CHAPTER 13
Don't Go Alone

If you want to go fast, go alone.
If you want to go far, go together.

This is not an opportunity to go start your own little homo-spiritual house church.[1] I'm not a big fan of the typical house church attitude. Many times, house churches bring together people who are against something, or who are running away from something. One or two families holing up together and having a pity party doesn't constitute a thriving church. Uniting around common grievances is a recipe for disaster.

Instead, the goal should always be continual aggressive church growth and division. Too often those

---

[1] homo-spiritual: spiritual fellowship with others who think like you.

of us with enough vision to break the status quo and start a new church are also pretty idealistic. Strong ideals can make it difficult for us to work with others. Hopefully we as a culture will normalize starting new churches. Then anyone could initiate a new church instead of only the freethinking, idealistic visionaries.

Committees often lead to stalled projects and safest common denominator thinking. There is a 'play it safe' factor in human nature that is often manifested in committees, boards, and governmental bodies. This destructive tendency drags corporations, churches, and state run institutions down to mediocrity and irrelevance. I want to be careful about recommending a committee because committees are often where ideas go to die.

But a small, diverse advisory board can be a big blessing to a new congregation. And this advisory board can help take the edge off of the aloneness a new church may feel. An advisory board for a new church can help mitigate some of the difficulties of navigating new brotherhood relationships. A new congregation could choose three or four brothers from a different congregation to counsel and advise for the first several years.

You should also hope to begin a new church with a minimum of three or four families. You need their support and diversity. Don't go alone. A lone sheep is a dead sheep.

One common reason to go alone is to avoid the complications of team relationships. We can move faster alone. One of the reported benefits of going alone is that it can force you to connect sooner with people in the area. But we are not the body of Christ alone. A body takes members. And members are people. No matter how gifted you are, you are not gifted enough to start a church by yourself. Maybe you go alone because you want to be the leader. Jesus said the leaders in his kingdom would be servants. Start serving your church if you want to be a leader. You do not need a title to sweep the floors.

A big reason to not go alone is practical. You may with great difficulty be able to start a church only through converts. But why? Starting with a small group of families can give you a thirty-year head start (versus starting alone). If you are committed to perpetually dividing and starting new groups your church could reach far more people by repeatedly sending out a small group of families than by sending one person out from a large group. And three or four families create a more resilient core. You will have the opportunity to show your new neighbors how beautiful it is when brothers dwell together in unity.[2]

We live in a world where everyone seems to be pushing something. Jehovah's Witnesses and Mormons knock on your door. Baptists wave signs and scream

---

[2] Ps. 133:1.

biblical damnation from the street corners. Norwex, Melaleuca, Conklin, and drugs are recommended by "friends." Billboards advertise everything from whiskey and cigarettes to the love of God and warnings about hell. We are the most advertised-to culture that ever existed. *The world will rest their advertisement weary eyes on your little group of families and observe with interest how you present the gospel in your daily lives.* Talk is cheap. Presenting a living gospel with your families and daily lives provides social proof and authenticity that words cannot match. And a group can do this much more effectively than one family.

    Another consideration is your emotional health. Missionaries burn out. Trying to build a church is difficult work. Failure and rejection are daily challenges. Mental health suffers. Religious mental cases are everywhere. Church, family, and friends can help us deal with these setbacks. As we suffer together, we build deeper relationships which in turn strengthen the church. We need each other.

    Don't go alone. A lone sheep is a dead sheep.

Chapter 14
Become Native

He who puts his hand to the plow and looks back is not worthy of the kingdom.[1]

Put your hand to the plow and do not hope to return. Plan to become a native in the place you are going. You are not going for a two year or a twenty-year term. You are going for life. Of course, we are all somewhat transient, aging parents need care, churches fail, jobs come and go, financial situations change, people die, and many more reasons beyond our control come up to cause us to relocate. I understand that these dynamics exist. But that is quite different from leaving for the mission field with the intention to return. We must shift our thinking from transient to native.

---

[1] Luke 9:62.

JESUS AND THE MENNONITES

When our forefathers came to the Americas they did not intend to return to their motherland. When they waved goodbye to their aging parents, they never expected to see them again. And most of them never did. The Moravians came as resident missionaries, and they were a brilliant flash in the pan. The Anabaptists came as colonists, and today the faithful American population of Anabaptists is over 250,000. And this is not counting the churches in Canada, Australia, Central and South America, Europe and Mexico that were started by American churches. As far as I know, no faithful Moravian population exists today.

Almost daily reports roll in about unruly mission workers embezzling funds, taking advantage of vulnerable native children, impregnating neighborhood girls, and driving luxury "mission" vehicles, not to mention mental breakdowns among dysfunctional staff who don't speak to each other. Yes, similar things happen in the church, but not at the same scale. Churches are equipped to prevent some of these things. Much damage has been done by transient mission workers. In a healthy, stable home church environment, there are aggressive checks and balances. And by far the strongest of these checks and balances are long-term relationships.

The church by nature is relationship based. John said "If someone says, 'I love God,' and hates his brother, he is a liar."[2] Paul says we are "individually members of one another."[3] Part of being members of one another is to know each other's strengths and weaknesses. And that takes time.

Real relationships take lots of time. Many programs are intended to accelerate relationship development, but often these programs tend to emphasize an emotional feeling connection at the expense of a shared life experience bond. Research and experience have repeatedly shown that women are wired to form deep connections through warm conversation but men are particularly wired for connection through shared life experiences. In the context of church life this observation is critical. Deep ties that cannot be broken lie at the heart of solid churches.

Shared life experiences are undeniably the most powerful relationship builders on earth. This is why military personnel struggle to reintegrate into a society of frivolous relationships. They have shared misery, death, struggle, mission, and purpose with other men. Chatting at the coffee shop will never replace these experiences. Strong churches are built on sharing lifetimes together.

Plan to share your life, and your lifetime with the people you hope to reach. Do not plan to return.

---

[2] 1 John 4:20.

[3] Rom. 12:5.

> *"No one, having put his hand to the plow, and looking back, is fit for the kingdom of God."*[4]

---

[4] Luke 9:62.

CHAPTER 15
Think Logistics

Amateurs talk strategy and professionals talk logistics.[1]

Too often churches take the easy route. They split or divide and merely build another church house in the same area. This is the Achilles heel of Anabaptist churches. For some reason we have defaulted to this sinful pattern time after time. Very little has stifled the expansion of the living gospel more than our desire to pile up on the best farmland. We break away in the name of revival only to return like a dog to its vomit to the pattern of building a new Tower of Babel.[2]

Make a little effort to blaze a better path. So much energy has been wasted on adopting worldliness

---

[1] Omar Bradley.

[2] Pro. 26:11.

JESUS AND THE MENNONITES

in the name of cultural relevance. What a shame. We would be more culturally relevant if we were not surrounded by other plain people. All around the country communities have never really encountered the living gospel. How can they believe without someone to show them?

Look for places that are not already populated with Anabaptists. Some forward-thinking groups are looking to start new churches at least twenty miles away from existing Anabaptist communities. This is a great rule of thumb in rural areas. In urban areas, with their much denser populations, churches could be as close as a mile or two. But the concept is the same, do not build on another man's foundation. Develop close church communities, stop making long commutes to Sunday morning services the norm. And please do not default to driving into urban areas for "mission trips." Sometimes this is ok but the norm should be living in close proximity to the people we are trying to reach. It is so powerful to allow our neighbors to live life with us. They watch us, they see how readily we loan our tools, they see how our family gets along, we understand their joys and griefs, they observe our struggles and tragedies, and they begin to understand our living faith. They see that we are human, that we are not just more cheap gospel salesmen. But if we fight and bicker and devour one another then they will see that too.³ We really need to cultivate a deeper respect for our Anabaptist brothers.

Traditionally Anabaptists have moved to new areas in search of cheaper farms. Many rural communities have been revived by hardworking and frugal Anabaptist farmers. This is a good pattern that has served the church well. But too often we have stopped there. Farmland in the United States has gotten ridiculously expensive while farm commodity values have plummeted. As our communities are forced away from the farming lifestyles that have historically served us well there is much opportunity to be more flexible in our property choices. Many cities have seriously underdeveloped neighborhoods that need the living gospel. Paired with Anabaptist families who are skilled in construction, landscaping, gardening, mechanics, and many other practical skills these communities could become the new frontiers. *Imagine city blocks reclaimed from drugs, crime, drunkenness, trash, and crumbling buildings.*

Cities are intimidating to most Anabaptists. And for good reason. Cities have a life of their own. They are guarded by evil spirits. And we have no experience on this front. But God will go before us. He has made a way for His people throughout history. There is no reason to fear. We need people who will rise to the challenge. And we need people who are

---

³ Gal. 5:15.

JESUS AND THE MENNONITES

willing to really think long and hard about creative ways to occupy cities. Too often Anabaptists who move to cities quickly shift to higher education, consumerism, and sending their children to daycare. We can live in cities without adopting a worldly perspective, but we will have to be intentional. We need to continue to value working with our hands and being keepers at home. Think about ways to teach your children to value physical labor.

When you are considering areas to move to, think about living costs. In the country the best farmland is usually the most expensive. In the city the nicest neighborhoods are usually the most expensive. There is nothing wrong with starting a church in remote rural areas or in the slums of a city. It is easy to overthink our mission opportunities. We might dream of living where there is a Starbucks on every corner so we can witness to well-educated people over a cup of coffee. But we may be a much greater witness by operating a small grocery store or coffee shop in a community that has nothing but seedy gas stations, whether in dense urban areas or remote rural areas. We think we need two hundred acres of prime farmland to keep our families safe. *But far more plain children have been killed in farm accidents than by stray bullets.* And the massive debt required to maintain these farms has destroyed many families.

Remote rural areas often have depressed economic opportunities. Land is usually less expensive but making money is also more difficult. Do not let that deter you. People living with less economic opportunity are usually much more receptive to the gospel. Let us reclaim the wilderness. I want to see churches in the wilds of Alaska, in the swamps of Louisiana, in the hollers of Appalachia, in the sands of Florida, on the islands of Hawaii, in the deserts of Nevada, on the plains of North Dakota, in the slums of St. Louis and Chicago, and everywhere in between.

To be fast, successful, and replicable we need to figure out how to make this work with no mission board, no large financial backers, no long-term support church, no long-term volunteers or interns, and no loss of godly culture. This requires finding uncomplicated and inexpensive ways to move forward. I have heard of groups who sent out new churches with a starter fund. Others have merely provided advice and volunteer labor. Others have provided blessing and prayer support. Any of these can work, let us not get bogged down with details, finances, and committee meetings. Remember, we want this to be simple enough that the new church can replicate in a few years. And we want to fail quickly, so we can learn quickly. *Too many external props can prolong an unsuccessful project for decades.*

Another practical consideration is diversity of gifts. You need the brother who is interested in inexpensive property or new business opportunities just as badly as you need the brother who is looking for mission opportunities. *The fatal flaw of many new churches is catering too much to the missionary minded.* This leaves the new church fatally lopsided. Many practical cultural practices decline rapidly without a good diversity in the church. The uncomely parts of the body are essential.[4] Without practical minded members intent on living the gospel, churches can quickly become nothing but quarrelsome, freeloading evangelists with inflated views of their own importance. Welcome diversity lest you become "wells without water."[5]

One massive logistical challenge for new communities is schooling. State laws have become increasingly restrictive on education. Most states have a few homeschooling loopholes that Christian families have been able to exploit. We need to continue to be creative in finding ways to give our children a good education without being unnecessarily expensive or time consuming. Sometimes homeschool co-ops may serve our educational needs better than regular Christian day schools. Homeschooling can also be an option but may be unnecessarily time consuming for busy mothers. Sharing at least some of the schooling load is usually healthier. Keep in mind that the majority of the state required schooling time in public schools is spent in recess and extracurricular activities.

---

[4] 1 Cor. 12:23.

[5] 2 Pet. 2:17

Do not worship education; it must keep its place as a God-given tool. "Without education, we are in a horrible and deadly danger of taking educated people seriously."[6]

On a final note, I rarely recommend someone switch churches. But if you are in an area that is overrun with Anabaptists it may be worth considering moving to another area. Hopefully you could join with a group moving to a new area. But for many of us that is not immediately possible. We may need to first spend time with a group that has a passion for intentional division. Please don't use this as an excuse for church hopping. Spend time in fasting and prayer and it just may be that God has placed something in your hand that you are not yet aware of. Maybe there are others in your group with a passion for starting a new church, and you could do this with the blessing of your group.

Uncomplicated, inexpensive, and replicable. Think simple, move quickly, welcome diversity. *"The meek shall inherit the earth."*[7]

---

[6] G. K. Chesterton, *"The Illustrated London News,"* December 2, 1905.

[7] Matt. 5:5.

AND NOW...

CHAPTER 16
Powerful Prayer

Because of your unbelief.[1]

So Jesus said to them, "Because of your unbelief; for assuredly, I say to you, if you have faith as a mustard seed, you will say to this mountain, 'Move from here to there,' and it will move; and nothing will be impossible for you. However, this kind does not go out except by prayer and fasting."[2]

I have spent a lot of time warning you about the dangers of hyper-spirituality. And the danger is real. But now that we have addressed the fallacy of the worldly interpretations of faith, let's take a deeper look at real spirituality. *We would be greatest fools to go into new territory without a robust dependency on God.* Some

---

[1] Matt. 17:20.

[2] Matt. 17:20–21.

men in Acts 19 tried that and they fled naked and wounded.[3]

We need prayer—lots of prayer. Prayer is our communication with God. What many Christians have wrong about prayer is that they think it is an easy substitute for obedience. But we know from Proverbs that the prayers of a person who ignores God's rules are an abomination to Him.[4] We need faith and works.

So, as you dream of areas to conquer, pray. God does not desire long, fancy, public prayers. He can do mighty things through the prayers of old people, too feeble to kneel. He can work through the simple prayers of simple people. We constantly underestimate the power of prayer. God will do mighty things through His people; He wants us to ask. Let prayer be your all-consuming attitude throughout the day. Pray for churches. Pray for converts. Pray for cities, states, and countries. Pray for people willing to go.

One thing we often misunderstand is the power of evil. We believe, and rightly so, that the victorious resurrection of Jesus defeated all evil powers. The problem is that in many areas of the world satanic forces are alive and well. Fake Christianity has hardly dulled the grip of evil in these areas. The demons of lust, murder, bloodshed, unbelief, darkness, and hate have long ruled these areas and they are not giving up

---

[3] Acts 19:16.

[4] Pro. 28:9.

territory easily. Daniel, the powerful prophet, prayed three weeks until the angel was able to come to him.[5] This is a man who walked away unharmed from the den of lions! I believe prayer is part of a chain of cause and effect set up by God. I think the prayers of the saints have a cumulative effect. Just as in the story of the unjust judge,[6] we must be persistent for our prayers to be effective.

Righteousness breeds righteousness and evil breeds evil. In areas where the demons of evil have bred unchecked for generations, we will need extra spiritual power to invade. We must be committed to prayer and fasting if we wish for God to drive out the enemy before us. I believe that part of the reason Satan has so successfully corralled God's people into a few areas of North America is *because of our lack of prayer and fasting.*

"And nothing shall be impossible for you."[7]

---

[5] Dan. 10:2–3.

[6] Luke 18:1–18.

[7] Matt. 17:20.

CHAPTER 17
Do It

We no longer lack vision; we lack the will to execute.

Often when new ideas are presented we stall because we desire more information. The unknown is scary. So, we wait. And wait. And wait. And slowly forget. Cares of this world, the deceitfulness of riches, and the desires for other things destroy our will.[1] Easier alternatives present themselves.

Satan silently circles our camps, terrorizing those who would step out in faith and leaping on the naïve who dare try to invade his territory. He magnifies the doubts within us and amplifies the voice of our critics. His reign of fear is effective. We are scared. Our faith is too small. We run back to our idols of structure. And Satan is pleased—very pleased.

---

[1] Mark 4:19.

But beyond the raucous crowds of Babel, away from the golden calves, beyond the family farm await glistening fields of opportunity. God is offering you the opportunity to be a co-laborer with Him. Dust off your swords, pick up a map, and follow your fearless Commander. I believe God is intensely interested in seeing new churches started. He is excited about His bride. *He wants you to help expand His kingdom.* It is your calling.

At some point we can no longer prepare, we must go. We no longer lack vision; we lack the will to execute.

Go spread your trophies at His feet.[2]

---

[2] Edward Perronet (1726–1792).

Afterword

I have a dream: what if we stopped fantasizing about short-term missions and instead started placing churches in strategic locations?

I want to start Anabaptist churches in Hawaii. I would like to see American Anabaptists invading and occupying every city and every state in the United States. Some parts of the United States are supporting toxic populations of Anabaptists. We have exceeded our carrying capacity and are left to fight and bicker over limited resources. Our communities have become tourist attractions and crime centers. Loss of purpose and the depression that follows plague our communities.

Does the message of this book resonate with you? Are you thinking of ways you and your church could move out the stakes of the tents of Jacob? Do you have a vision to start a church in a new area but do not know where to start? Would you like to connect with others who share your vision of kingdom expansion? Is your church doing something that you would like to share with me? I would love to hear from you.

Hector Troyer
210 Limerock Terrace
State College, PA 16801
hectorltroyer@gmail.com

Hector is passionate about church expansion. He is the busy father of five boys and one girl, their ages ranging from two to fifteen years old. He and his wife Lois currently live in State College, Pennsylvania. They are praying towards starting an Anabaptist church in Hawaii.

Recommended Resources

Batterson, Mark. *In a Pit with a Lion on a Snowy Day.* New York: Multnomah Publishers, 2016.

Bercot, David. *The Kingdom That Turned the World Upside Down*, Amberson, PA: Scroll Publishing, 2003.

Byler, Ted. *The Mystery of Christ in the Revelation.* Berlin, OH: TGS International, 2009.

Kreider, Alan. *The Patient Ferment of the Early Church.* Grand Rapids, MI: Baker Academic, 2016.

Kuruvilla, Finny. *King Jesus Claims His Church.* Cambridge, MA: Anchor Cross Publishing, 2013.

Miller, Gary. *Church Matters.* Berlin, OH: TGS International, 2018.

S2S Books is a project of Strength to Strength, which is committed to  advancing Jesus' kingdom by assisting the church in earnestly contending for the faith that was once for all delivered to the saints. We do this by tackling thought-provoking topics, by stimulating candid discussions, and by sharing faith-building testimonies.

Visit our website for a live roundtable of the Strength to Strength team discussing the history and vision of this initiative.

strengthtostrength.org/roundtable/

To listen to roundtable audio by phone, call (712) 432-8776, enter conference ID number 5555#, and sharing ID number 9144#.

Visit our website for a live interview where Hector shares the story behind this book.

To listen to interview audio by phone, call (712) 432-8776, enter conference ID number 5555#, and sharing ID number 9147#.

strengthtostrength.org/s2s-books-01/

Questions or comments: contact@strengthtostrength.org